By Marisa J. Taylor
Illustrated By Fernanda Monteiro

Diversity To Me

Text & Illustration Copyright © 2022 by Lingobabies

Written by Marisa Taylor

Illustrated by Fernanda Monteiro

ISBN: 978-1-914605-21-5 (paperback)
ISBN: 978-1-914605-22-2 (hardcover)

Edited by Shari Last

All rights reserved. This book or any portion thereof may not be reproduced or used in any manner without the permission of the publisher except for the use of brief quotations in a book review.

DEDICATION

This book is dedicated to all the children of the world who feel insecure about their differences. May you learn to love and embrace what makes you different from the rest.

Every day tell yourself one thing you love about yourself and always remember that you are perfect just the way you are.

This book is also dedicated to my children, who I love dearly. You inspire me to be a better person and to use my voice to stand up against racism & inequalities.

Marisa Taylor

Hi, what's your name?

....

Do you know the word "diversity"?

Let me tell you what that word means to me.

**Diversity is about being different:
A different look, a different culture, a different race.**

A different ethnicity - even a different face.

Everyone is born different,

and that is a wonderful thing.

Because if everyone was born the same,

the world would be boring.

I have curly hair, brown skin,
and freckles on my face.
But that's not what defines me.
It's my joy and style and grace.

My friend Ore is different, too: he is not like me. He is shy and quiet - the kindest kid you'll ever see.

Alexia is different, too.
She loves to paint and run.

She's the fastest kid I know.
Together we have such fun!

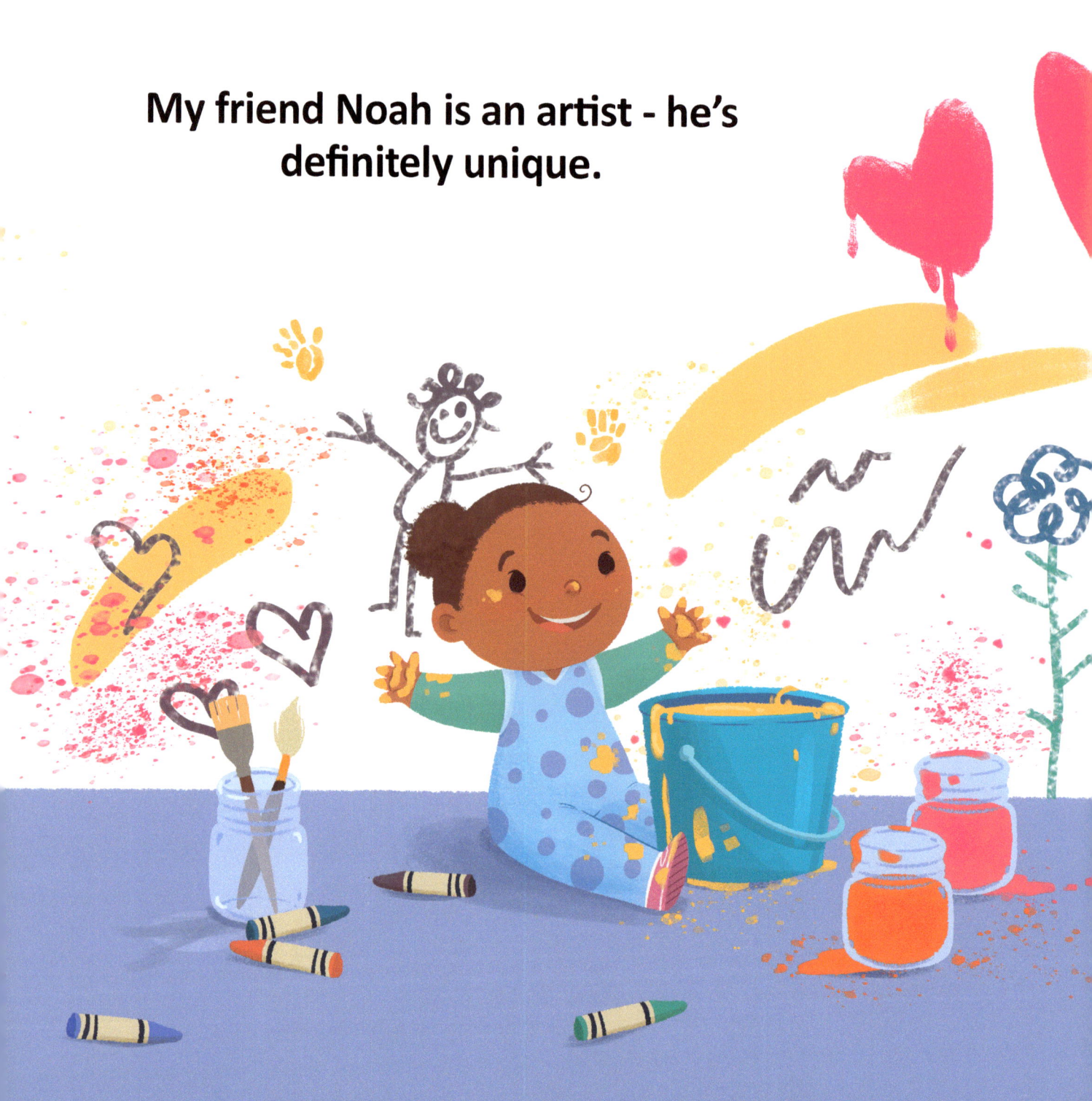

My friend Noah is an artist - he's definitely unique.

He's also such a joker,
I laugh each time we speak.

We all are beautiful!

We have special powers to offer the world, and that is our story.

We should never judge someone for who they are, but accept them in all their glory.

Our physical, cultural, and religious differences make the world a beautiful place.

Differences are beautiful,

and are there for us to embrace.

Everyone has their own special talents. That's what makes us shine - you and me.

About the creators

Marisa Taylor is a German/Canadian Author who resides in London, UK with her husband and children. They are a multiracial & multilingual family. Marisa has always been interested in learning & teaching languages, as she feels that it is the key element to connecting with people from other cultures. After becoming a mother she saw the lack of diverse resources available and became passionate about creating diverse bilingual resources that encourage children to celebrate multiculturalism and to learn a second language.

Instagram: @lingobabies

Fernanda Monteiro is a Brazilian illustrator and a mother of two, Íris and Aurora. She graduated in journalism, but her dream was always to work with drawing and found that the best way to do this would be through creating illustrations for children's books. Fernanda believes that through art she can contribute towards a better world in the future.

Instagram: @fe.monteiro_art

English-Spanish bilingual books

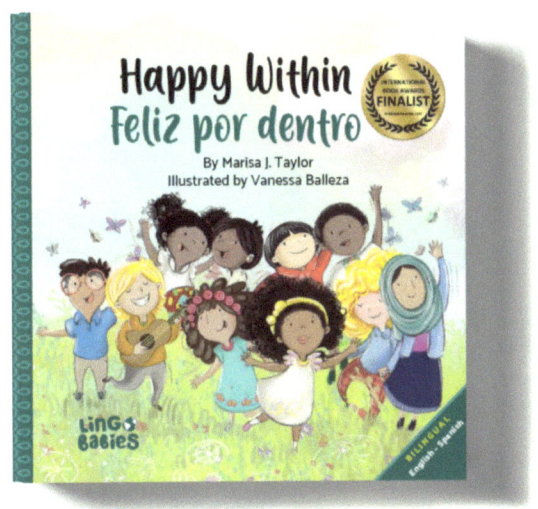

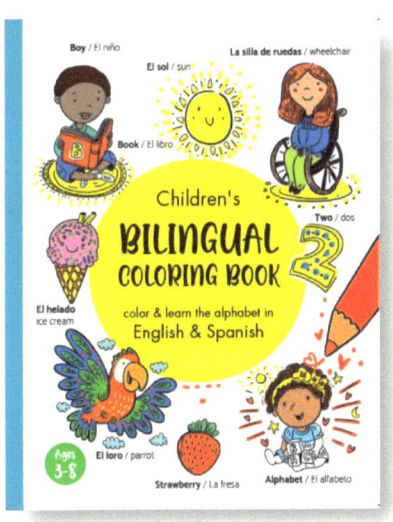

www.lingobabies.com

www.ingramcontent.com/pod-product-compliance
Lightning Source LLC
Chambersburg PA
CBHW041500220426
43661CB00016B/1206